WRITTEN FOR TEACHERS BY TEACHERS!

THE ULTIMATE BEHAVIOR MANAGEMENT MANUAL

Managing an Educational Environment in the Modern World

Tyran Payne M.Ed. and Ryan Stone B.A.Ed.

Copyright © 2023 Tyran Payne, Ryan Stone.

All rights reserved. No part of this publication may be reproduced, distributed, or transmitted in any form or by any means, including photocopying, recording, or other electronic or mechanical methods, without the prior written permission of the publisher, except in the case of brief quotations embodied in critical reviews and certain other noncommercial uses permitted by copyright law. For permission requests, write to the publisher, addressed "Attention: Permissions Coordinator," at the address below.

ISBN: 979-8-9877408-0-4 (Paperback)
Education

This manual is intended to be used for educational purposes. The content contained in this manual are suggestions from experienced teachers. These teachers have been trained in many techniques and strategies. Any similarities to published information is not intended to be a violation of copyright. We direct our readers to the information they can research to find out more about specific products.

Printed in the United States of America.

Cover design and layout by Victoria Wolf, wolfdesignandmarketing.com.
Copyright owned by Tyran Payne and Ryan Stone.

First printing edition 2023.

Cedar Hills Publishing
19462 Rolling Hills Rd
Warsaw, Missouri, 65355
www.cedarhillspublishing.com

CONTENTS

About the Authors 7

Acknowledgments 9

Contributors Page 11

Introduction 13

PRIMARY GRADES (PK-2)

Anxiety 18

Blaming 20

Bothering/distracting other students 22

Denying misbehavior 24

Emotional outbursts 26

Inappropriate language 28

Not paying attention/following instructions 30

Poor communication skills 32

Refusal to complete work 34

Seeking attention 36

Talking back 38

Talking out of turn 40

Throwing fits 42

Unable to sit quietly 44

Understanding personal space 46

INTERMEDIATE GRADES (3-5)

Arguing/fighting 50

Disrespectful of others learning 52

Ignoring directions 54

Inappropriate language 56

Lack of listening skills 58

Low educational stamina 60

Missing social coping skills 62

No self-control 64

Poor motivation/lack of effort 66

Refusing to do things 68

Sexually inappropriate behavior 70

Stealing 72

Talking back 74

Talking out of turn 76

Texting inappropriate content 78

MIDDLE SCHOOL (6-8)

Arguing/fighting 82

Attention seeking behavior 84

Disrespect authority 86

Dress code violations 88

Gives up easily on hard tasks 90

Inappropriate social media use 92

Inappropriate sounds/noise/talking 94

Lack of parental help 96

Lying/cheating 98

Misuse of cell phones 100

Not completing classwork/homework 102

Refusal to work 104

Repeating negative behavior 106

Sleeping in class 108

Talking back 110

HIGH SCHOOL (9-12)

Disregard deadlines 114

Do not complete make-up work when absent 116

Dress code violations 118

Grades not motivation for doing work 120

Inappropriate language 122

Lack of effort 124

Leaving class for different reasons 126

Misuse of cell phones 128

Misuse of social media 130

No parental support 132

Not following directions 134

Poor attendance 136

Sleeping in class 138

Talking back 140

Will not sit and work quietly 142

APPENDICES

Classroom Expectations 146

Voice Level Chart 148

Zero Voice Level 150

Funny Stories 153

ABOUT THE AUTHORS

TYRAN PAYNE is in his 28th year in public education. He is currently the Behavior Interventionist at John Boise Middle School in Warsaw, Missouri. Ty is a former principal at the secondary level. He has also managed many classrooms throughout his education career. Having taught over 20 different subject areas in his teaching career, he has many different educational experiences. Being trained in: Positive Behavior Intervention and Support, Response To Intervention, Capturing Kid's Hearts, and extensive training with Dr. Spencer Henry, has shaped Ty's philosophy on classroom behavior management.

RYAN STONE is in his 7th year in public education. Currently he is teaching 5th grade music at the Sedalia Middle School in Sedalia, MO. Ryan taught K-8th grade music in Warsaw, MO to begin his career. This is where he met Ty Payne. Before his teaching career he taught lessons and worked in a music store all through college. He is also a staff member at his church where he teaches children, youth, and leads the worship team on Sunday mornings.

ACKNOWLEDGMENTS

I (TYRAN) would first of all like to thank my wife, Amanda for all of her love and support as well as lending her knowledge to this project. I would also like to thank my mom, Sandra. A lifelong educator that taught me the value of education and the importance of being an educator. Mom also taught me through her example how to manage a classroom. I want to thank Ryan Stone for his work in collaborating on this effort and having a great initial idea. Thank you to all of the members of my family that have given your lives to education in service to others. I love you all. Thank you to those that have mentored me. I appreciate you pouring into me and shaping me into the educator I am today. Finally, thank you to all of those that answered the survey to get the ball rolling on this project. A huge thank you to the experienced educators that took the time to share your wisdom and be a contributor to our manual.

I (RYAN) would like to thank Tyran Payne, a veteran teacher, for helping a first-year teacher. If it was not for him, I would not be the teacher I am today. His guidance led me to this idea to help struggling teachers like myself, learn from experienced teachers. Thank you for helping make this dream into a reality and collaborating to make this idea even better. I also want to thank my wife Kirstin for all the love you give me and for encouraging me to use my gifts that God has given me to help others and teach. Thank you to my grandfather for taking me to music lessons and instilling your life lessons into me. Your words and wisdom meant more than you know. I also want to thank my family for giving me a wonderful home in which to grow up. I love you! Finally, I too would like to thank everyone who answered the survey and those who took the time to share their knowledge in our manual.

CONTRIBUTORS PAGE

A HUGE THANK YOU to the following educators for contributing their knowledge to this project. Also, thank you to many educators that contributed knowledge but chose not to have their names printed.

- Kelsi Brosnahan
- Sarah Cramer
- Megan Daleske
- Shellene Dore
- Doug Duncan
- Pride Goodloe
- Amanda Payne
- Laurie Poyser
- Sharla Shannon
- Amy Spunaugle
- Bobbi Swisher
- Cynthia Trout
- Richelle Wilson
- Sue Yates

INTRODUCTION

THE PURPOSE OF THIS MANUAL IS TO HELP EDUCATORS that are struggling with behavior management in their educational settings. Two lifelong educators have collaborated to bring you an easy to access manual of ideas from experienced teachers. This project began with researching the issues educators are having in the return from COVID 19, educational environment. This research took place throughout the United States covering thirty-four states in the union. Of the educators surveyed, ninety-two percent agreed that behavior management was becoming increasingly difficult. The fact that so many people, in so many areas of the country, were experiencing behavior management issues in their classrooms led us to move forward with this manual. We took the top 15 most mentioned issues from the survey for each grade level. It is definitely our desire that this will give you some good, practical ideas. This manual is intended to help not only those preparing to teach, those new to teaching, but also those veteran teachers that may be struggling.

Using this manual is simple. All you need to do is look at the contents and find your teaching level. Primary grades are Pre-K through second grade. Intermediate grades are third grade through fifth grade. The Middle School grades are sixth through eighth grades. The High School grades are ninth through twelfth grades. Once you have found your grade level in the contents, then you find the issue you are dealing with in class. Turn to the page that corresponds with the page number in the contents. You will find on that page, five different suggestions from veteran teachers that will help you in your classroom. On the facing page are boxes that contain information "from the authors." These commentaries will give you valuable information to further help your classroom behavior management. There are also spaces for you to take notes. In addition, there are appendices at the back of the manual to help specific situations that you might encounter as a teacher. Thank you for choosing this manual, it is our sincere hope that this will change behavior management in a positive way for educators.

As you begin to use the great solutions in this manual, there are some universal truths that apply to all educational environments. The following five items are things that every teacher, in all settings, needs to have in their behavior management toolbox. If you learn these five things alone, you will be well on your way to the classroom manager that you want to be.

- ***Know your expectations***
  In order for you to manage your classroom, you must establish expectations for all procedures that will take place. From how to line up, to how and when to sharpen your pencil, you will need a plan for everything. Even at the secondary level, this is important.

- ***Teach and practice your expectations***
  Do you know one of the biggest differences between successful classroom managers and unsuccessful managers? Teaching and ***practicing*** classroom expectations until the students know them inside and out. Teaching expectations should be done just like you would, when teaching content.

- ***Be consistent everyday***
  You must follow through on every expectation, every single day. If you are not consistent, the students will know that and you will have more problems on your hands. You must be firm, fair, and consistent.

- ***Get off the see-saw***
  This is my way of saying, "There is never a good time to get into a back-and-forth power struggle with a student." When you were a kid on the see-saw, you would go crashing to the ground if the person on the other side jumped off. In other words, there can be no power struggle if there is only one willing participant. Classroom management is not about winning, it is about compliance. "For the love of everything sacred, get off the see-saw!"

- ***Do not take misbehavior personally***
  Students misbehave for a variety of reasons. They will often test your patience. Even when it seems like it is personal, it is not. This is difficult to do, but you must always remember it. While they might be testing you, it is not personal toward you.

PRIMARY GRADES
(PK-2)

ANXIETY

- Have a variety of "objects" that your students know they can get when they are anxious: fidgets, stress balls, etc.

- Have a small weighted blanket that students can use.

- In the room, have a tent/cabin that the highly anxious students can go into when nothing will calm them down.

- Find a way to activate the student's proprioceptive system. Use: joint compression, weighted vests, a squeezy hug etc. to calm them.

- Use alternative lightning as opposed to standard overhead LED or fluorescent lights.

FROM THE AUTHORS

Having students feel comfortable and safe in your classroom is very important. Many students new to the school setting experience nervousness. In the COVID world, children have experienced trauma that we have not seen in the school environment. As teachers it is a necessity that we understand that some of the behaviors we see are a result of trauma. If your school has an occupational therapist, ask them for strategies that you can use in the classroom to help calm anxious students. They can be a great resource.

NOTES

BLAMING

- Explain to students that they cannot control other people, only themselves.

- Have the student write down their story of what happened, then discuss with them the results.

- Ask them, "If I look at the cameras, what will I see?"

- Question the student on their role in the incident. "What did you do when that happened to you?"

- Have them role play and model how they should have reacted in that situation.

FROM THE AUTHORS

This is another situation where students might be tempted to argue. The best strategy is to walk away and disengage. Do not have a conversation with the student until they are ready to accept responsibility for their actions. This is a "get off the see-saw" moment. When you do not engage in a back and forth, students learn to better take responsibility.

NOTES

BOTHERING/DISTRACTING OTHER STUDENTS

- Have the student go and sit away from the class.

- Send the student to a predetermined room where they can finish their task.

- Give them a "satellite" space in the room. This separates them from others, but keeps them engaged.

- Have them use a fidget or attention directing device to keep them from distracting others.

- Teach them KAHFOOTY. (Keep All Hands Feet Other Objects To Yourself)

FROM THE AUTHORS

At this young age, it is possible that students are not trying to be malicious in class by being a distraction. They may simply be reacting in a social situation, or they may be seeking a classmate's attention. It is important to correct this consistently and be caring about it. If you do have a situation where the student is being malicious and distracting students on purpose, that must be stopped. The five suggestions here will help you to curtail students that are preventing learning in the classroom.

NOTES

DENYING MISBEHAVIOR

- Stress to the student the importance of taking responsibility for their actions.

- If a student is not ready to talk, walk away. "I can see you are not ready; I will come back when you are."

- Refer back to a classroom expectation and have them read it and explain how they did not follow it.

- Send them to a pre-established "buddy" room that is a grade younger or a grade higher. Make sure to send an assignment to work on and a time to return.

- In 1st or 2nd grade, have them write out what they did and then read it back to you.

FROM THE AUTHORS

If a student is willing to deny their misbehavior, they must be kept separate from the group until they are willing to accept their actions. Anything other than admitting what they did and apologizing keeps the student from the group. Until they are ready to have the conversation and apologize, they need to be isolated from the group. This teaches them to take responsibility for their actions. Consistency is also a key in this situation.

NOTES

EMOTIONAL OUTBURSTS

- Remove the student to the hallway (away from an audience) and try to calm them down.

- Encourage them to take deep breaths. (Research Conscious Discipline calming breaths.)

- Teach them the Brain Gym Hook-Up. (Research how to do this.)

- Have a safe place in the room for the child to go to self-soothe.

- Have a stuffed animal they can cuddle.

FROM THE AUTHORS

It is very important that you try a strategy and if it does not work have someone available to remove the child. You cannot allow this behavior to disrupt the entire class. Each day, practice self-calming strategies with the entire class. If they have practiced it every day, they are more likely to be able to effectively use the strategy in crisis. The goal is to teach a child to self-regulate in the educational setting. Sometimes they are not taught this at home.

NOTES

_____
_____
_____
_____
_____
_____
_____
_____
_____
_____
_____
_____
_____
_____

INAPPROPRIATE LANGUAGE

- Use it as a teaching moment. The child may not know what the word means and is repeating what they have heard.

- If the language is bad enough an office referral is warranted.

- Have them restate what they said with appropriate language. The real young ones may need help with proper wording.

- The first time simply tell them that is not a word we should be saying. They may not know it is inappropriate.

- Call the parent and have the student tell the parent what they said.

FROM THE AUTHORS

Students at this young age that use inappropriate language have heard it from someone in their lives that are older. It is important to make them aware that what they are saying is not language that someone their age should be using. Make sure you do everything you can to prevent this in the future. You do not want other students in the class to start repeating the inappropriate language.

NOTES

NOT PAYING ATTENTION/ FOLLOWING INSTRUCTIONS

- Stand/sit with the child as close to you as possible.

- Eye contact is important. In some cultures, eye contact is disrespectful. Let your students know that NOT having eye contact/not paying attention is disrespectful.

- Try breaking the instructions up in 1-2 steps and have the students repeat them back.

- If it is ongoing, let the parents know, and document directly on the student's work.

- Redirect first, if it continues, change the child's location.

FROM THE AUTHORS

The younger the student the fewer steps they will be able to follow. Having the students repeat the instructions will help the students in the classroom that have slower processing. If you are busy, you can have a reliable student that other students can go to, in order to help with explanation. It is very important to make sure that students are learning to pay attention and listen to instructions in the educational setting at a young age. This will set the precedent for their future classroom learning.

NOTES

_____
_____
_____
_____
_____
_____
_____
_____
_____
_____
_____
_____

POOR COMMUNICATION SKILLS

- Have the nurse check their hearing.

- Give them time to complete their thoughts out loud.

- Say the statement/thought/question that they need to say (are working on) and have them repeat it.

- Let students hear your thought process on everything, whether it be a lesson or working through a situation.

- Make a referral to the speech therapist for receptive or expressive language delays.

FROM THE AUTHORS

Oftentimes what we teachers confuse as defiance or noncompliance, is a student's slow processing. Giving students time to work through communication is very important at this young age. For young students, teaching what a proper response looks like is important. Model how you would like them to communicate back to you and their classmates.

NOTES

REFUSAL TO COMPLETE WORK

- Use part (not all) of their recess time for them to work.

- Do not allow students to have independent play time in the classroom until their work is completed.

- Send it home as homework, after contacting the parents to let them know they have not been doing their work in class.

- Do not allow students to participate in center time, unless their written work is finished.

- Give them something meaningful to help them focus. "I had a rolling stool that was my personal stool. One student always wanted to sit on it but he would not sit and work. So, I made a deal that he could sit on it only if he stayed in his spot and worked on his assignments."

FROM THE AUTHORS

Searching for the cause of the student not completing the work is important. Is the student having trouble learning or are they just being defiant. Discovering the root of the incomplete work will help you know how to approach getting the child to be consistent with their completion of classwork. These five strategies can be very useful with those students that are simply being defiant and not working. It is important not to make the post assignment activity too fun, this can cause students to rush through or not complete work to get to the fun activity.

NOTES

SEEKING ATTENTION

- Give the student positive attention for positive things. Never give negative behavior positive attention.

- Remove them from the area where they are being a distraction.

- Send the student with a "note" to another adult (secretary, janitor, cook) in the school that they respond well to, and have them provide positive attention.

- Start the day giving them positive attention. (Nice outfit, nice haircut etc.) This will often sustain them through the day.

- Tell them, "now is not a good time." But, set aside a time later to give them one on one time.

FROM THE AUTHORS

Many students do not get the attention they need in their lives. They will often do anything to get attention whether it be positive or negative. With students at this young age, it is important to make a point to give them positive attention at appropriate times in school. It is equally as important to teach them there is a time and place to receive attention in a positive way.

NOTES

TALKING BACK

- Disengage from the student. Do not get into a power struggle.

- Explain that talking back is disrespectful and we are not going to do that in our classroom.

- Move the student to the safe seat.

- Tell them "I need you to stop talking and listen," (as politely as possible). If they do not, walk away until they are ready to comply.

- Raise your hand in front of the student. (This is the classroom signal for no talking.) If they continue talking, remind them the raised hand means stop talking.

FROM THE AUTHORS

The easiest way to stop talking back is to disengage and walk away. Walking away consistently teaches them that you are not going to engage in a back and forth, and that they are being disrespectful. It is important to teach the student ahead of time at the beginning of the year what it looks like when they choose to talk back. This will help them not be confused when you walk away and disengage. This is a "get off the see-saw" moment. If no one is on the other end of the see-saw, the back and forth cannot continue.

NOTES

TALKING OUT OF TURN

- Give students a blurt out limit. When the limit is reached, they are no longer allowed to talk.

- Allow two reminders to raise their hand, then they are assigned to a new area of the classroom away from the group.

- Give a visual cue to show students how you want them to answer. (Your hand up signals raised hand, two palms out signals group answer, etc.)

- Use the technique class class/yes yes (See Pg. 150).

- When a student blurts out, teach the class to turn to them and say, "No, thank you."

FROM THE AUTHORS

It is very important not to draw attention to the student for the blurt. They will continue to seek that attention. Acknowledging the students that are doing it correctly will help model for the blurting student. You must be consistent in dealing with the students talking out of turn in order to get them to stop blurting.

NOTES

THROWING FITS

- Try to stop the tantrum calmly and quietly, removing the child from the situation if possible.

- Model what is acceptable.

- Remove the other children while you calm the tantrum down.

- Teaching the student how to state what their needs are at the time (instead of the tantrum) is a key.

- If the tantrum is serious enough, use CPI techniques. (Research this program if you are unfamiliar.)

FROM THE AUTHORS

More students are crying out for help since COVID 19. With the younger students, the only way they have learned to do this, in many homes, is to throw a fit. Teaching appropriate claiming strategies is important here. It is also crucial to help students work through communicating their needs and feelings. Do not be afraid to utilize other adults in the building such as; counselors, occupational therapists, or behavior specialists if you have them. Maintaining good communication with parents will benefit you as well as the child. Having a team to work for the child's best interest will be an asset.

NOTES

UNABLE TO SIT QUIETLY

- Flexible seating - It must have firm guidelines and be managed properly.

- Some students have perched in their chairs.

- Allow some of your students to stand and work if they need to.

- Some students work better on the floor. If they are productive, allow them to do that.

- Move them to the back of the room.

FROM THE AUTHORS

Proximity is a key here. Have students close to you. If this is not possible, move the student away from others with whom they are having negative interactions. You can place the student with their back to the class to take away the temptation to entertain others in the class. You must set firm guidelines and boundaries if you choose to seat them with their back to the class.

NOTES

UNDERSTANDING PERSONAL SPACE

- Explain to the student the "personal bubble."

- Place a ring around your chair and they cannot step inside of it when approaching you.

- Teach and model appropriate social distance and have them practice, practice, practice.

- Have the student stand with their arms out and have them swivel at the hips side to side. Explain to them this is their personal space and others have that too.

- Help them to understand the spread of germs and illness.

FROM THE AUTHORS

The sweet little ones at this age just do not understand personal space. This, like everything else, must be taught. You as the teacher want to be careful as you teach them not to damage their desire to have a relationship with you. They are not invading your space because they are afraid of you, it is because they like you and are comfortable with you. It is very necessary to teach them about giving people personal space. Just do it in a loving way.

NOTES

INTERMEDIATE GRADES (3-5)

ARGUING/FIGHTING

- Have the "family talk" with them. Tell them they will spend more time with each other in your room than their own family at home. They need to treat each other with respect.

- If you have just a few students not getting along, move them apart. Put them in different groups and separate them as much as possible.

- Fighting at recess would lead to a restricted recess.

- Many students fight for other reasons than the fight itself. They may feel left out or be seeking attention. Fighting may be the only way they know to gain that attention.

- Have the two students that are fighting use affirming words about the other person (say what they like about them).

FROM THE AUTHORS

At this age, much of the arguing and fighting happens when they know you are not around or looking. Recess is the biggest problem. Make sure you know who to look out for and try to keep an eye on them. Arguing and fighting can be stopped by just your presence. Having a positive environment in your classroom will also help. Play fun games in your room to help the students get to know each other better. One of my favorite games is *I Have Never*. Try it out!

NOTES

DISRESPECTFUL OF OTHERS LEARNING

- Put them in a safe seat in the room.

- Talk to them one on one about how to act in the classroom and reteach how to act while learning.

- Reward other students for showing the correct behavior. Then, if their behavior changes, they can receive the reward.

- Restrict the individual learning environment and the student earns space as disruptions lessen.

- Students do not always realize they are being disrespectful to others' learning. Giving them examples may help them see and understand how their behavior disrupted others.

FROM THE AUTHORS

Every student is different in your classroom. Find out what will motivate them to learn. Be clear about rules, expectations, and consequences and follow through every time they are disrupting your class. If a student is showing this kind of behavior every day, start taking privileges away until they learn the expectations.

NOTES

IGNORING DIRECTIONS

- Have the students repeat the directions back to you, then repeat them again.

- Break down multi-step instructions and have the whole class repeat back what the instruction is.

- Have students circle the verbs in the directions so they know how many things they must do.

- Make the student go back and redo the assignment or task according to the directions.

- Go over the first direction with the student, have them repeat the direction, and then show you when the first step is complete. Then go over the next instruction and so on.

FROM THE AUTHORS

Get to know your students. Find out the ones you know who are going to need a little more help. A lot of time students are not ignoring you. Some don't understand and need extra help. Make it brief when giving instructions. Be specific and try to explain everything at once. Having the students tell each other what to do, after you have told the class, will also help the students that are struggling.

NOTES

INAPPROPRIATE LANGUAGE

- From the beginning of the year, let your students know what happens when they use inappropriate language. Do not ever let one slide.

- Avoid using inappropriate language in the class yourself.

- Often, students repeat what they hear at home. Speak with the student about their inappropriate language and if it becomes a real issue, call and involve the parents.

- Assign the student to sit by themselves at lunch.

- At recess, have the student walk the perimeter of the playground.

FROM THE AUTHORS

Students at this age should know better than to use this kind of language in class. If the language is an ongoing problem, you should let your principal know and ask what should be done. You will need to get more severe consequences if taking away recess and sitting them alone by themselves at lunch is not working.

NOTES

LACK OF LISTENING SKILLS

- Play a game of tic-tac-toe. Every time they talk, when you are talking, put an X on the board. When you are talking and they are listening, put an O on the board. If they win the tic-tac-toe game, reward that class with something fun.

- Identify the students who may need certain instructions repeated to them. Stop and ask them to repeat what was just said.

- Do lessons that involve listening skills. These are like games and they can choose from the prize bucket if they win.

- State the instructions, have the class repeat them, and then state them again in a fun voice.

- Talk softer on the important parts of the instructions to force them to lean in.

FROM THE AUTHORS

Before you start your lessons or give instructions use SLANT.

S: Sit up straight

L: lean your body toward the speaker

A: Ask and answer questions

N: Nod your head yes and no

T: Track the speaker with your eyes

NOTES

LOW EDUCATIONAL STAMINA

- Make your lessons relate to the students more.

- Use more technology in the classroom.

- Just printing an assignment on a bright or favorite color will intrigue a student long enough to keep going.

- Gradually add rigor to the curriculum beginning on the first day of school. This gets them in "shape".

- Add small brain breaks (stand and stretch, do a short rhythm song etc.) throughout the day in a self-contained intermediate grade classroom.

FROM THE AUTHORS

Part of being a teacher is making a lesson fun. Put your own spin on things to get students excited to learn. Expect achievement out of your students. Make sure they know your expectations in your classroom. Students should know what you expect, not only for behavior, but also for academic success. So students know what is expected out of them each day, have goals on the board.

NOTES

MISSING SOCIAL COPING SKILLS

- Talk to the school counselor and get ideas from counseling lessons to help the student.

- If a student has trouble coping, pull them aside to help them understand how to cope with the issue correctly.

- Teach the student "8 counts in, 8 counts out" breathing technique.

- Establish a safe place for the student to go to help them cope.

- Have the student, in a private setting, count backward slowly from 10 to 1.

FROM THE AUTHORS

Dealing with a student with no coping skills is hard to do in a classroom setting. Asking other adults to help or assist you would ease the burden. Engage in problem solving with the student. Ask them how they can fix the issue. You can also assign another student in the room to help them and be their friend.

NOTES

_____
_____
_____
_____
_____
_____
_____
_____
_____
_____
_____
_____

NO SELF-CONTROL

- Restricted area of learning. Tape an area on the floor near the teacher. The student can be in that area only. As days progress and behavior improves, the tape moves out.

- Consistently acknowledge those that are doing the right thing. Most of the time the ones who are having trouble focusing will get back to work because they also want to be noticed for doing the right thing.

- Have the student do some breathing/yoga style exercises to help center them.

- Send the student on an "errand" to get them out of the room. This will help them come back ready to work.

- Allow them to do odd jobs in the room if they prove they can control themselves.

FROM THE AUTHORS

Help your students avoid temptation by putting them in a safe environment. Keep things that will tempt them out of sight. Make sure they know the classroom expectations and reward them for consistently showing self-control.

NOTES

POOR MOTIVATION/ LACK OF EFFORT

- Talk to the student one on one. Find out what they like and offer a simple reward for completed tasks.

- Try teaching the subject in a different way. Use things students enjoy in your lesson.

- Talk about things that are going on in today's world and relate it back to the lesson.

- Shorten tasks/assignments.

- Break down multiple step instructions for the student.

FROM THE AUTHORS

Apathy has become a problem in all levels of education. This trickles down to students. There are schools of thought both for or against the concept of rewards. I feel like if you have a way to motivate an unmotivated student, then you should use it. The fact of the matter remains, if you are not able to get students to be motivated in your classroom it is going to be hard to teach them anything. Using these strategies can help to reach the part of the student population that is unmotivated.

NOTES

REFUSING TO DO THINGS

- Give the student a choice: You can do _____ or you can do _____. Even if both options are something they don't want, just giving them a choice makes them feel that they have some sense of control.

- Have a plan in place if they refuse to make a choice, like a person (counselor, principal, etc.…) to call that can remove the student.

- Many times, students like these have an IEP or behavior plan, check to see what protocols are in place.

- Ask questions, find out if they have help at home. This helps you help them. If they know that you are on their side, you tend to get more out of them.

- Put them on a "Yes only" program where they must meet any requests.

FROM THE AUTHORS

This is a situation where you must try to get to the root of the problem. Establishing a relationship with the student will help you in this area. Students at this age choose not to work for different reasons. If it is a lack of understanding, then that is different than just being defiant. Once you determine the cause, you can adjust accordingly.

NOTES

SEXUALLY INAPPROPRIATE BEHAVIOR

- It is possible the student does not know what they are referring to and needs a conversation with an appropriate adult outside of class.

- Report it. If it keeps happening, report the inappropriate behavior to your school counselor.

- At this age, this is an indicator of a more severe problem. It needs to be reported to a social worker or counselor.

- Always involve the parents, counselor, and the principal. This is a very delicate subject that you should never handle on your own.

- Immediately remove them from the situation and call one of the administrators.

FROM THE AUTHORS

Much of the time students in this age group make sexual noises or say inappropriate things. They get these ideas from social media, or on the bus with the older students. In my experience, most of the students do not know what they are saying. In today's society we are forced to educate students on things outside of our content area. In this situation, it is often best to let someone else in the building explain the content of their behavior to them.

NOTES

STEALING

- Find out why the student is stealing. Are they stealing because they don't like someone or because they need something?

- Develop a relationship with the students and find out their needs, but also follow up with the appropriate punishment within your school's handbook.

- When a student is caught stealing, they should be required to make amends with the person from whom they stole.

- Make the right things easy and the wrong things hard. If you ask the right questions, you may find out why they felt they had to steal.

- Contact the parents and make arrangements for the items to be returned or the cost worked off.

FROM THE AUTHORS

Stealing is a situation that indicates other issues, in many cases. Often, students that steal feel left out or like they do not have things others have. It is extremely important to your classroom environment that this be handled well and that students feel comfortable and safe in class.

NOTES

TALKING BACK

- Talk to this student one on one. Find out their favorite candy and tell them if they treat you and their classmates with respect you will give it to them at the end of class.

- Say "I don't argue with ____ graders". Repeat every time they say something, use a calm voice and keep your body language relaxed.

- In a one-on-one conversation, ask "Did what you said make the situation better or worse? What would be a better way of handling that?"

- Do not engage in the power struggle. Calmly explain to them what you need them to do and disengage.

- Offer them two options. Stop or explain to their parents and the principal why they made this choice.

FROM THE AUTHORS

If you have a student talking back to you, they do not respect you. Never let a student get away with talking back and make sure they are being respectful. Remember, how you talk in class influences how they talk. Model what you want from them at all times. If the problem keeps happening, talk to the student one on one. Most of the time, they are talking back to get the attention from the rest of the class. This is a situation for "get off the see-saw." If you have ever ridden a see-saw with someone and they have you at the top and they get off, you go crashing to the ground. The back and forth cannot continue with only one person on the see-saw.

NOTES

TALKING OUT OF TURN

- Use a point system. Every time they talk out of turn the class loses a point. Have an end of the term prize. Make it a mystery. If you tell them what it is, some of the students might not care. Try making a mystery box.

- Try to ignore- even negative attention is attention to them. Later, you can have a private conversation with them about their behavior.

- Stop having students raise their hand - use popsicle sticks and draw out a name to answer a question.

- Use hand signals, number of fingers, response cards to represent different responses. (Nothing audible.)

- Call on students one by one with no hand raising.

FROM THE AUTHORS

Make sure the students know from day one your classroom expectations. Tell them what will happen every time they talk out of turn, and be consistent with consequences. When they do not do it correctly, make them start again to practice. When they do raise their hand to talk, praise them for it. Always give positive feedback to those doing what you want them to do.

NOTES

TEXTING INAPPROPRIATE CONTENT

- Make the students leave their phones in their lockers.

- If phones are allowed in your building, make them put them in a basket when they enter the room.

- Take phones if you see them and return them at the end of the day.

- Always involve the parents with these issues, some parents allow their children to do this. Parent support is the key in any situation, especially this.

- Have the student explain what the content means (in a private conversation). Often, they have no idea what they are saying.

FROM THE AUTHORS

You cannot control what the students do outside of your classroom or at home, but in your class, you are in charge. No intermediate school student needs a phone in class. This is just an unnecessary distraction. I believe all schools should have a universal cell phone policy. This gets to be an even bigger issue as they get older.

NOTES

MIDDLE SCHOOL
(6-8)

ARGUING/FIGHTING

- Sit down with both parties alone, do a mediation, and let each of them talk.

- Ask the students involved if this is worth getting into trouble in school and possibly legal trouble.

- Separate the students' seating as far as possible.

- Use it as a teachable moment about debate. Have them write cases and turn in their arguments. Try to get them to understand proper argumentation.

- If the fighting turns physical, Call for the SRO (School Resource Officer) or Principal.

FROM THE AUTHORS

Arguments can escalate very quickly in middle school. You must put an end to this at the very beginning of the situation. If you do not, it could become a physical altercation in your classroom before you have time to stop it. That is the last thing anybody wants. If you are not able to calm the situation, get your administration involved as quickly as possible.

NOTES

ATTENTION SEEKING BEHAVIOR

- Seat these students in the back of the room in an attempt to isolate them, but still include them in the regular desk formation.

- Make sure there is "coincidentally" an empty desk beside them, or a quieter student who doesn't get distracted so easily.

- Try to reduce downtime as much as you can and keep things moving along.

- Make sure to have a more structured and rigid class time when you have these types of students in class.

- Try asking them to wait until the end of class, when we usually have about 3-5 minutes to spare.

FROM THE AUTHORS

Students in general want positive attention in school. All of them want it for different reasons. Try to establish a relationship with students. Find out what motivates them. If the attention seeking behavior is distracting the rest of the class, you must put a stop to it. Try to get the student to understand that you cannot give all students individual attention all of the time. Try to make a connection with the student to get them to see your side of the situation. Give them as much positive feedback and attention as the structure of the class will allow.

NOTES

DISRESPECT AUTHORITY

- Give them a one-word directive "stop" with direct eye contact and their name. If they continue, send them to the hallway and have a one-on-one conversation.

- Have a one-on-one conference with the student and talk to them about why you want them to be successful and respectful.

- Earn their respect by treating them firmly and fairly. Maintain your structure in your classroom.

- Ask questions, try to understand why the student is disrespectful first, then try to correct and be understood.

- Give each student 3 strikes. (Strike 1- Politely ask them to fix behavior, Strike 2- Call home, Strike-3 detention and call home, office referral after that.)

FROM THE AUTHORS

Never allow a student to be disrespectful to you in your classroom. This will cause the other students in the class to think they can do it as well. Address this problem immediately. Do not allow the conversation about the situation to happen with an audience. It is highly likely that the student being disrespectful is allowed to do that outside of school. If you ever let it go, then you are giving permission for it to happen again in the future. If necessary, get your administration involved. Most of these five suggestions are what to do at the beginning of the disrespect. This is a "get off the see-saw" situation. Do not engage in a back-and-forth argument with a student. If there is no one to argue back, an argument cannot happen. Remember, it is not about "winning." It is about behavioral compliance.

NOTES

DRESS CODE VIOLATIONS

- If it is a minor violation, wait until the end of class to speak with the student about it.

- Make sure to resolve it immediately if it is a major violation, but still maintain discretion so as not to exacerbate the situation.

- Have someone in your building who handles dress code violations. Send the student to them, so they can make sure the student changes.

- Have a designated "School Store" with extra clothes if a student should need to change.

- The principal keeps gray sweats and shorts, along with plain gray t-shirts and hoodies for dress code violations.

FROM THE AUTHORS

This is a very tricky situation. The best solution I have seen in buildings is to have a designated female in the building that handles dress code violation discussions. This is usually the school nurse. This is a person that can have a conversation with both females and males. It helps them to find out if there is a problem with the student's ability to get clothes or if they are just defying the school dress code. It also allows for a discreet conversation to happen so as to not embarrass the student.

NOTES

_____
_____
_____
_____
_____
_____
_____
_____
_____

GIVES UP EASILY ON HARD TASKS

- Establish an environment where it is ok to make mistakes, and let students see that you make mistakes too.

- Keep your thumb on them and make sure they are working. To do this you must be able to monitor all of them.

- Celebrating success is the best way to motivate them to persevere through a hard task and have the confidence that they can do it.

- Try to break the task into smaller, more manageable parts.

- When there is a multi-step task to be completed, it will frequently look like a difficult task. Talking the student through the steps one at a time will often convince the student that the task is not as hard as they have perceived it to be.

FROM THE AUTHORS

If a middle school student gives up on an assignment, most of the time it indicates that they do not understand and are feeling "dumb" or inadequate. It is important that you show them you care about their success. These 5 suggestions can be very effective in this situation.

NOTES

INAPPROPRIATE SOCIAL MEDIA USE

- Monitor student chrome book use through Lightspeed. (This is a classroom observer program.) You can see if they are on an inappropriate site and freeze their screen.

- If there is misuse on social media, regardless of the nature of it, send them to the office to talk with the principal.

- Position yourself where you can see if a student is misusing their chrome books or using their phone in class.

- Have the student do their work with paper and pencil only. They must write everything out, no electronics.

- Have the technology department block the ability to use social media.

FROM THE AUTHORS

Social media is a problem in our society. While it does have its merits, it can be a vicious tool. I believe that schools should have a policy and take the steps necessary to prevent all social media access in the school buildings. There is no way you can monitor what students do outside of school. But in the building, all precautions should be in place. If your school does not have a policy, have discussions with your administration about it. Make sure you follow the chain of command. Start with your building level administration first.

NOTES

INAPPROPRIATE SOUNDS/ NOISE/TALKING

- The first step is always a redirect. Give specific directions to stop the behavior and remind them what the classroom should sound like.

- Speak to the student privately in the hallway and remind them of the classroom expectations.

- Remove them from the classroom if severe enough. Having a constant distraction in the classroom is not fair to the others who are trying to learn.

- Use proximity control (Walk over and stand beside their desk and keep teaching.). If they still continue to talk, ask them if they are done. At that point, they will become quiet and usually embarrassed or frustrated.

- Very directly tell them to stop and say their name.

FROM THE AUTHORS

This is a very common problem in middle school. This is again established on the first day of expectations. You must really be consistent with this one. Each time there is a problem you must correct it and stay on top of it. If you do not, the noise and inappropriate talking can get away from you very easily. You cannot allow students to be a distraction from another student's learning.

NOTES

LACK OF PARENTAL HELP

- Structure your class so that students will have 20 minutes to start "homework". Go to those struggling and they can ask specific questions.

- Make a video of you teaching every lesson, so students can access it at home if they forget what to do.

- Several students from over the years voluntarily check in periodically. These students are seeking a "Mom" or "Grandma" to take an interest in them. That's what you need to do.

- Our school created parenting classes for the district. Make sure the student's parents are aware of these classes.

- In the most tactful way possible, have a conversation with the parents to explain their help is needed and wanted.

FROM THE AUTHORS

Unfortunately, this is becoming an increasingly bigger issue across education. Whether it is because parents are too busy or they just do not care, the problem persists. This is an area where relationships are super important. Do your best to understand the situation the student is going through. Try to find out how you can help them and show them you care. This does not mean that you do not hold them accountable. You need to make sure that you communicate well with the student. These suggestions from teachers are great ways to help this situation. Talk to colleagues that have handled this situation well to see what they did.

NOTES

LYING/CHEATING

- If you catch students cheating, divide the one grade by the number of students that cheated, and they all get that same grade.

- Cheating is an automatic zero in class and they know it from day one.

- Follow the student handbook on this violation.

- Have the student redo the assignment in front of the teacher.

- First, have a private talk with them about what you saw happen. They can either redo the assignment or take the F. Offering some extra help/support can go a long way in helping a student feel like they have the ability to do the assignments on their own.

FROM THE AUTHORS

In my experience in middle school, I have found that a lying or cheating student has underlying problems. It could be that they did not have time to study or that they do not understand the content. It could be that they do not care. Whatever the reason, you cannot tolerate lying and cheating. However, you can deal with the situation in a positive manner. The student must still face the consequences of their choice. It is not necessary to make them feel less of a person because of the mistake.

NOTES

MISUSE OF CELL PHONES

- Use a hanging pocket chart (for calculators) which serves as a cell phone storage center.

- Treat cell phone misuse like passing notes in class. If they are on it, take it and give it back after class.

- Have a basket where students place their cell phones when they come to class.

- If you hear it or see it, take it. Return it at the end of the hour.

- All students must place their cell phone in a caddy in the office. If they are caught with a phone during the day, it is taken. Their parents must come get it and pay a $15 fine to get it back. (This is a school policy.)

FROM THE AUTHORS

Cell phones have become inherent in our society; therefore, everyone believes they have a right to have them anywhere. This is simply not true, especially in the school setting. I firmly believe that all schools should have a universal policy on cell phones in their buildings. If your school does not have a universal policy, then take steps and talk to the administration and try to get that ball rolling. If your building has a universal policy, for goodness sake, follow the policy! Nothing is harder for administration than teachers that know policies and do not follow them.

NOTES

NOT COMPLETING CLASSWORK/HOMEWORK

- Assign after school tutoring. When parents have to come pick them up it motivates them to do better.

- Give students time for independent work in class and do not assign more work than what can be done within 30 minutes of independent working time. (This is for 45-minute classes in the schedule.)

- Structure the class so that you lecture, show examples, and do informal assessments for 30 minutes and they have 20 minutes in class to work and ask questions. (This is for 50-minute class periods.)

- Have the student get their lunch tray and come to your classroom to complete their work.

- Use a shared "buddy" room (Another classroom designated to send students to.) for the student to go to and work.

FROM THE AUTHORS

This has become an increasingly difficult problem in middle school. I strongly suggest that you rethink the homework concept. The vast majority of middle school students will not complete assigned homework. You will find yourself beating your head against the wall to get it turned in. I went to classwork only and monitor the students very closely as they are working to make sure they are not misusing their time. These suggestions are very good ways to conduct a middle school working environment.

NOTES

REFUSAL TO WORK

- Talk to the student one on one to find out what they do not understand. Show you care.

- In a one-on-one conversation, listen to why they are not working. Pick out the "good" stuff in their reason and focus on that. Talk through why it would be good to do some of the work.

- Explain to them the importance of working even when they do not want to. Sometimes you too do not want to teach every day, but you do.

- Accommodate the work in order to get some participation. Any completed work is better than none.

- Have good behavior sticker charts in your class. Each day a student has good behavior and completes their work, they get a sticker on their chart. Stickers lead to rewards. (Middle schoolers really do like it.)

FROM THE AUTHORS

Defiance in the classroom is at an all-time high. For many reasons, students refuse to do things. In this situation, as with many others, the relationship you have built with the student comes into play. They need to know that you understand their situation but that you need them to do the best that they can for you each and every day. Establish in your expectations that you want the best they have to give every day. That may mean that they can only give you 40 % on a particular day, but you want all of that 40%.

NOTES

REPEATING NEGATIVE BEHAVIOR

- Talk to the student individually and encourage making positive choices over negative choices.

- Explain to them that when they choose not to follow the expectations, they are putting you as the teacher in the position to discipline them.

- Use three strikes and you are out. On the third time they go to the office.

- Assign them detention if they continue to repeat behaviors that have previously been corrected.

- Have the student explain to you what it means to be successful and point out to them they are not doing that.

FROM THE AUTHORS

Middle school students are going to need corrections time and time again. You as a teacher must understand that. I have always said that teaching middle school is 90% classroom management and 10% content. You can never tire of managing them properly. Every time they are not meeting expectations, you must correct it according to what you establish on the first day of class. Eventually they will understand that you are serious, and they will fall in line. There will still be situations that arise, but they become fewer as the year moves on. I call this proper front-end loading. Do the hard work at the beginning, so that it will get easier as the school year goes on.

NOTES

_____
_____
_____
_____
_____
_____
_____
_____
_____

SLEEPING IN CLASS

- Try to wake them up without drawing attention from the rest of the class.

- Make changes, such as seating them up front, or closer to your desk.

- Keep the temperature pretty brisk in your classroom in order to keep everyone a little more alert.

- Examine lecture strategies you are using which might make students fall asleep, and make attempts to reduce downtime and monotony.

- Make habitual sleepers stand at the back of the classroom.

FROM THE AUTHORS

Take a caring approach on this one. It is likely that students are having an issue outside of school that is causing them to be extra sleepy. It is very easy to take this personally. It may seem as if they are bored in your class. Take the time to try to understand the root of the problem. This can also help you to establish a relationship with the student.

NOTES

TALKING BACK

- Stop it in its tracks, and definitely do not give in to engaging with a back-and-forth.

- Try to find the reason behind the action and assume there is something more going on.

- Make sure they know you care about them, want what's best for them, but will not ever tolerate that negative behavior in your classroom.

- Remember that it's not personal and give them the benefit of the doubt that they are having a bad day. Give them the chance to explain.

- DO NOT allow yourself to get heated or engage in an argument in the middle of class.

FROM THE AUTHORS

This kind of disrespect cannot be tolerated in the classroom. If you tolerate talking back, this will lead to more severe disrespect not only from the initial student but from their peers as well. Have a conversation with your principal and work out a discipline plan if it continues to be a problem. This is another situation where you need to "get off the see-saw." Never engage in a back-and-forth argument with a student. This is often easier said than done. Nothing good comes out of having an argument with a middle school student.

NOTES

HIGH SCHOOL (9-12)

DISREGARD DEADLINES

- Accountability!!! Stick to the due date and its consequences.

- Document everything, provide all the information at the front end so the student has no questions about due dates and/or policy.

- Hold them accountable by sticking to the policy; otherwise, they will not respect the deadline.

- Keep your word, even on things that they may view as "punishment"; this shows them they can trust you.

- Every school and teacher is different, but whatever you set as your policy you MUST stick to it.

FROM THE AUTHORS

As a teacher, you must be an example of accountability. You must do things on time and be on time yourself. It is only then that you can expect a high school student to do things on time. Once you set the deadlines, you must stick to it every time. The first time you let it slide is the time you lose them adhering to deadlines. Consistency is super important to students at the high school level.

NOTES

DO NOT COMPLETE MAKE-UP WORK WHEN ABSENT

- Utilize folders that are titled with the assignments. Leave them in a designated place and students know when they are absent, they need to check the folder for that assignment.

- Put the grade in as a zero.

- If possible, email the student their assignments when they are gone.

- Put in the syllabus the policy on absent work and talk about it from day one. Make sure they know when they return to school the work they need to complete.

- Post a video on Canvas of you teaching the lesson and their assignment.

FROM THE AUTHORS

It is super important that students understand your policy on make-up work and the procedures therein. This needs to be covered the first day of class and it needs to be followed consistently from that day, for the rest of the year. If you are inconsistent, they will be inconsistent.

NOTES

DRESS CODE VIOLATIONS

- Do not embarrass a student, but do address this according to the school policy.

- Relate it to the work environment in the future. If a job required a specific dress code, it would be for a reason, and to their benefit to adhere to that.

- Send the student to the designated person to handle school dress code violations. This can be done without the student knowing, through email.

- Try to find out if the student needs help getting appropriate clothing to wear.

- Our assistant principal has clothing in school colors that say dress code on them for students to change into.

FROM THE AUTHORS

High School students often know when they are in violation of the dress code. They like to push the envelope to see what they can get away with. This is also one of those things that must have consistency. It is never a good idea to embarrass a student. You might have the situation where the student truly had nothing else to wear and are just lucky they made it to school in the first place. Treat them with dignity, even if you think it is intentional.

NOTES

GRADES NOT MOTIVATION FOR DOING WORK

- Sometimes they simply do not understand. Do the work with the students and only give them a short assignment that can be completed quickly in the classroom.

- Students that are not motivated by grades are generally motivated by time. Take up their time (before school, after school, during lunch), they will get some work turned in to you.

- Show them that they have many opportunities in their future. Help them find the resources they need to get there.

- Work something out with one of the student's elective teachers and have the student come to your room instead, even if it is for 10 minutes.

- Everything should be negotiated between you and the student, not parents. It develops an understanding that they alone are responsible for their work and holds them accountable.

FROM THE AUTHORS

Finding ways to motivate students can be very difficult. This also goes back to building a positive relationship with the students. If students know you care about them, they are more likely to work for you. These 5 things can help you find their motivation for working. Finding this answer is a huge key in unlocking their inner drive. Many times, students need a structured environment. They live in chaos and need a teacher that cares enough to give them consistency and support.

NOTES

INAPPROPRIATE LANGUAGE

- Ask them to choose a different word and stand there until they do.

- Students learn the expectations for inappropriate language from day one. Compare the expectation to a future job they are trying to get. We are trying to develop you for life after high school.

- If it is a slip of the tongue, no big deal. If it occurs again, Send them to the office.

- Explain to the student that using curse words is easy. It takes a much better vocabulary to use sophisticated words.

- Assign them a detention, as long as the language is not directed at the teacher or someone else in the class.

FROM THE AUTHORS

High school students believe they should be able to use whatever language they want. This is simply not true. There are certain words that are not acceptable in public and it is up to us as teachers to teach them that. It is important to model the type of language that you want your students to use. Let them know on the first day of school what is acceptable in your class and what is not and be consistent. Closely monitoring your own language will help.

NOTES

LACK OF EFFORT

- By understanding the reason for the lack of effort, you can better motivate them.

- The best way to overcome this mindset in struggling students is one-on-one to begin with.

- Engage students and help make connections for them from their personal experience.

- Work through the assignment/activity right along with them. Help them step-by-step. Correct and redirect as needed, but praise all along the way.

- As you move around the room make sure to stop and encourage them in a way that does not make them feel "stupid", but may even help them "show off" what they do know.

FROM THE AUTHORS

High School students face a variety of problems from a variety of angles. Having a positive relationship with your students is very important in this situation. If you have a positive relationship with them, they are likely not to fall into a lack of effort. If they do, you can approach them to see what is going on. However, it is possible that a student simply is not wanting to be in your class or work for you as the teacher. This is something that you must deal with in a positive way also. While you cannot allow students to be in class and not working, it is best to try to understand what they are going through outside of school to understand why they are not trying. These are 5 good suggestions for you to try.

NOTES

_____
_____
_____
_____
_____
_____
_____
_____
_____
_____

LEAVING CLASS FOR DIFFERENT REASONS

- If they give reasons that seem legit, investigate! Find out if they are telling the truth.

- Talk to other staff members and make sure they are not "helping" them leave class.

- If a student is claiming a medical reason, double check with the school nurse.

- Do not let them leave.

- Give them a limited number of times they can leave class in a week.

FROM THE AUTHORS

This falls into the category of just say NO. If a student seems to be finding every reason in the world not to be in your class, you must not allow them to leave. If they insist it is super important, stand your ground. Be consistent! They may initially get mad at you, but they will respect your consistency. All 5 of these suggestions are things I have done before in my own classroom.

NOTES

MISUSE OF CELL PHONES

- Correct this with your location (proximity). Go stand behind them.

- Use a calculator caddy (Amazon) and assign each student a number. Put this number on the class roster, so students use the same number all year.

- If you see it, take it. Students know this from day one.

- Treat it like note passing. If it is a problem, take it up and give it back at the end of class.

- Many schools have a universal policy that needs to be followed. Be consistent!

FROM THE AUTHORS

Cell phones have become an increasingly bigger problem. In our initial survey of high school teachers, 100% of them listed cell phones as one of their top three problems. In my opinion, schools should be going to a universal school-wide policy. If your school is not doing that, you should approach administration as to their thinking behind not having a universal policy. If your school does have a school wide policy, you MUST follow it consistently for it to be effective. If you let kids slide with the policy, it not only weakens your discipline stance. It also weakens the policy itself. This puts those that enforce the policy in a negative situation with students. You expect students to follow your expectations, in turn, you must enforce the school-wide policies.

NOTES

MISUSE OF SOCIAL MEDIA

- Have the IT department block the student's social media.

- Managing student cell phones properly in class will prevent them from having access to social media. They can use the chrome book provided to them for work.

- Do not "friend" or follow students on social media, so you don't know what they are posting.

- Do not allow cell phones in your class. They must be silent and not visible. Students know that if you see a phone on top of their bag or desk, you will take it and turn it into the office. Be consistent!

- Give one warning. After that, take whichever device they are misusing in order to be on social media.

FROM THE AUTHORS

Students should not be on social media in the classroom for any reason. If you allow this to happen, you are opening up a can of worms that you cannot get back into the can. Management of this starts from the beginning of the year and students knowing the policy. Be firm with following up on the expectations. If your school does not have a school wide policy, you should talk to the administration about instituting one.

NOTES

NO PARENTAL SUPPORT

- Starting at the beginning of the year, make positive email contact with the parents.

- Mail home a beginning of the year letter. It explains the importance of the parents' and students' roles in your class.

- Try to support the student in as many ways as possible.

- Make at least 5 positive communications home before having any negative communications.

- Stay strong, make sure you can defend every action you have taken with their child. Most of the parent's frustration is caused by their own child, but they sometimes misdirect it towards teachers.

FROM THE AUTHORS

This is the sad state of all levels of education. We have parents that are self-centered and do not care about the education of their children. If they do care, more than likely the students are not in trouble and are thriving. The best approach is to be as supportive as possible for these kids. Try to fill a hole in their lives. You will never be able to be their parent, but you can help them in a way that will teach them to be a self-sufficient adult. The truth of the matter is, sometimes other things are more important than the content you are teaching. It is easy to forget that, with all of the pressure put on us as educators.

NOTES

NOT FOLLOWING DIRECTIONS

- Follow through with whatever the consequences may be for not following directions.

- Make them do the assignment again.

- In your syllabus, designate an amount to reduce their grade for not following directions and stick to it.

- Repeat directions often. As many times as it takes.

- Give them random assignments that say read all of the directions first. Direction number 2 will say go to the last question. The last question is, put your name on the paper and turn it in.

FROM THE AUTHORS

This may come as a surprise, but high school students do not listen well all of the time. I know, bombshell, right?! Use little "games" in your assignments to help them to pay attention. It can be a fun way to get them to follow instructions. In working for several school districts in several capacities I have learned that teachers do not follow directions sometimes too. Give your students the same grace that you would like extended to you. Use these 5 suggestions with dignity. You never want a student to feel "stupid" just like you as a teacher would never want that yourself.

NOTES

POOR ATTENDANCE

- Make sure the parent/guardian is aware.

- Talk with the student, find out the "why" if possible and work from there.

- Have them come in outside of class to make up for missed work or instruction.

- Try to convey how much you want that student to be present for class.

- Keep them after school for make-up work. If they don't drive, parents hate having to pick them up.

FROM THE AUTHORS

This becomes increasingly difficult as students get above the required age for compulsory attendance laws. The truth is that most states in the union have juvenile offices that are overrun and the last thing on their list is making sure high school students that are underage are going to school. All you can do is the best you can do. Try these 5 things and make the student see the importance of an education. This again can be difficult, especially if you live in an area of the country where a student can go to work and make more money than you as a teacher.

NOTES

SLEEPING IN CLASS

- If they cannot stay awake, have them stand.

- Get them up and moving, engaged.

- Have them lead the activity or lesson that is going on in class.

- Send them on a quick errand to get them moving.

- Make a loud noise to wake them up.

FROM THE AUTHORS

You simply cannot allow students to sleep in your class. If you do, you are discounting the importance of the class. If they are sick or need to rest, find another place other than your classroom to get rest. The relationship aspect of teaching comes into play here as well. If you have worked to establish a relationship, students will be open and honest with you about what is going on. In turn you can usually be honest with them.

NOTES

TALKING BACK

- Disengage from the student. Do not get into a back and forth.

- Simply tell the student "That does not work on me," then walk away. Address the issue later.

- Try very hard to listen to what they are saying and understand the meaning of the back talk. The main thing is not overreacting and speaking in a kind tone, no matter how you feel.

- If it is mild, make a joke of it, "like whoa, whoa, whoa - I don't think you meant that to sound that way, let's start over" and literally start the whole conversation over again.

- Say, "excuse me?" in a polite tone. If they say never mind, it's over. If they repeat it, immediately dismiss them to the hallway and tell them to wait by the door until you come out and speak to them.

FROM THE AUTHORS

I say, "get off the see-saw." If you have ever been on a see-saw and one person gets off, the other person goes crashing to the ground and they can no longer see-saw. If you completely separate from the student, the back and forth cannot continue. You must maintain your composure. Much of the time they are trying to get you to "lose it." If they can make that happen, it is a win for them in their eyes and others will try to get to you as well.

NOTES

WILL NOT SIT AND WORK QUIETLY

- They do not get the privileges that the other students get when they choose their seats. Assign them a seat based on how they are behaving.

- Allow students that need to move around to refocus (not misbehave) to do so.

- From the beginning of the year establish a way to get zero voice level (no sound, see pg. 150) and stick to it and use it consistently.

- Stand near a student to help redirect frequently. If this is disturbing the learning of others, Send the student to the office.

- Assign them time with you (detention) outside of class.

FROM THE AUTHORS

Even at the high school level, it is important to establish a zero-base voice level in your classes. In the appendix of this manual on page 150, there are six suggestions of how to do this in a classroom. You must be consistent with this and do it every time you need the class quiet. At the beginning of the year, high school students need to be trained in this and all expectations. Teach this just like you would teach your content. Just because they are older, that does not mean they do not need to be trained on expectations in the classroom!

NOTES

APPENDICES

CLASSROOM EXPECTATIONS

- Example # 1
  - Be On Time
  - Be Prepared
  - Be Courteous

- Example # 2
  - Be Respectful
  - Be Responsible
  - Be Ready and Safe

FROM THE AUTHORS

IT IS VERY IMPORTANT that you use the word expectations. If you use the term rules, that has a negative connotation to students. The word rules is daunting to the good students that want to do things correctly, especially if there are too many rules to follow. To the student that is a troublemaker, the word rules indicate something to break.

In your classroom when you create expectations, they need to be short and to the point. The two examples here are very good. The first one covers things that can happen in the classroom and you can redirect students toward the expectation. The second one is actually my own classroom expectations from my last year in the classroom. These are based on the school-wide behavior initiative that we started in our building.

If your building has a school-wide initiative, it is important that the students hear the same use of vocabulary throughout the building from the different adults they may come in contact with. This helps to create consistency in what the students are hearing.

When creating your list of expectations, it is important that you know from day one what you are going to be teaching the students. You need to teach them about how they meet each expectation. For example, I did not just tell my class they were expected to be respectful. I taught them exactly what it meant to be respectful in my classroom. I broke it down into sections of the expectation. When other people are talking, give them your attention. Stay in your seat if we are in the middle of a lesson. Restroom and water breaks need to be taken during independent working time. Manage your own things you bring into the classroom. Use polite and courteous tone. Follow the school student handbook while in class. These examples fit into the category of being respectful. I taught this expectation from day one and I made sure that I enforced that expectation until the last day of school. You will need to establish a list for every expectation that you teach and practice with your students. Yes, middle and high school teachers you need to do this. It will help your classroom management tremendously!

VOICE LEVEL CHART

- 0- No Sound

- 1- Whisper

- 2- Talking one to one

- 3- Talking to a group

- 4- Talking to a large space

- 5- Yelling only in an emergency

FROM THE AUTHORS

This voice level chart is a great way to get students at all grade levels to understand the importance of vocal awareness. In your classroom, it is hard to teach if the volume is too high and the students cannot hear you. On the other hand, in most classrooms there are times noise is necessary. Teaching and practicing the voice level chart will help with students understanding when and how much the volume can increase.

NOTES

ZERO VOICE LEVEL

You will need to establish a set way to get a voice level zero. Below are some suggestions different teachers use.

- Teacher says, "class class" and the students repeat "yes yes" followed by zero sound.

- Teacher holds up their hand and the students repeat the gesture as the teacher counts down from 5 to 1 with a zero sound at 1.

- Teacher uses a rhythmic clap that is repeated by the students with zero sound following.

- A hotel bell is rung followed by zero sound.

- A whistle is blown followed by zero sound

- A trigger word like "BOOM!" is used and all students stop and listen with zero sound.

FROM THE AUTHORS

All of these suggestions work if they are taught and practiced by the students. The teacher must also use the chosen suggestion consistently in order to establish the routine of having the zero-sound level. The chosen method for zero sound level also goes along with the voice level chart from the previous pages.

NOTES

FUNNY STORIES

ONE OF MY MIDDLE SCHOOL STUDENTS that almost always had good behavior was sent to the office for fighting with another student. After the office trip, in a very serious state of mind, he said, "I know what's wrong with me today Mrs. Shannon. I figured it out. I'm going through puberty today."

I TAUGHT FORENSIC SCIENCE for a few years. We were in the middle of our fingerprinting section and the students were taking turns fingerprinting their partners and analyzing the characteristics of fingerprints. A group went to the restroom to wash their hands. Later in the day the principal called me and asked me what we were doing in class. I told him we were fingerprinting. He said that one of the students basically walked down the hallway to the restroom walking his fingers down the wall. I ended up using their assignments to figure out which student it was so that we could take appropriate disciplinary action.

I ONCE TAUGHT in an amazing science classroom/lab. It was a huge room with the classroom desks at the front of the room and the lab tables and all the cabinetry for storage was at the back of the room. In the very back of the room, there were a set of double cabinet doors to a cavernous lower cabinet.

I still had elementary aged children at the time. I was a coach as well as teacher, so we spent a lot of time at school and couldn't take off easily. I threw blankets and pillows into that cavernous cabinet, so my children had a place to "nap" when we were stuck up there for a long time.

One day during school, one of my children was not feeling well so they came to my classroom and climbed into the cabinet to nap. This thing was huge. They closed the cabinet doors and fell asleep. Meanwhile, my class came in and we went to work. I never shared that I had one of my children sleeping in the back of the room. During class, we were working in the lab area when suddenly the cabinet doors flew open and a sleepy kid stretched as if all was normal to everyone else. Students jumped, screamed, jolted away from the cabinet! I could not have scared them better if I tried.

After that, I had students requesting to "nap" in the cabinet for the rest of the year. :)

WHILE TEACHING SCHOOL in Tuntutuliak, Alaska, I could only speak English. My students were bilingual and English was a second language. I thought I was being clear about the directions to a math problem and I asked the students if they understood. No one answered me. I was quite puzzled. I ask again and still no answer. I finally asked one specific student why no one was answering and he told me that they were answering, but I just didn't see them answer. I found out that they use facial expressions to answer questions. The raising of eyebrows is yes and the lowering of eyebrows is no. I felt quite silly.

WHILE WORKING AT A SCHOOL in South Texas, I had recess duty. I am not a fluent Spanish speaker, but I try. I told this little girl, while pointing at her feet, "Me gusta tu changos." to which she and her friend died laughing. I asked them what was wrong, why were they laughing? The other little girl said, "You just said you liked her monkeys." We all had a good laugh. The Spanish word for flip flops is chanclas.

I WAS TEACHING A LESSON in geometry one day in my math class. The question was, "What is the area of a square with a side measure of 5?" A student came up to me frustrated because the problem did not give the other measure they needed for the area. I tried, to no avail, to explain that it is a square. A few days later the light bulb came on and that is what teaching is all about. I never gave the student the answer. I allowed the student to struggle because to this day this same student remembers this problem and the answer to the problem.

BE CAREFUL with your April Fool's Day pranks. One year I brought in caramel dipped onions, covered in nuts. It was quite funny watching the students take the plunge into them, until one of them thoroughly enjoyed it and finished the entire thing. I'm not going to lie; it was terrible to smell for the rest of the day.

MIDDLE SCHOOLERS can be sneaky. I went about my day teaching in my classroom all day like normal until I got to 6th hour. Two of the girls came into my classroom laughing and asked me if I noticed anything different in my room. Of course I didn't, I was going about my day. They seemed disappointed and told me to just take a really good look around my room. Once I started looking around, I noticed what they were talking about. These girls snuck into my room sometime in the morning and stuck googly eyes on everything! My projector board had them, my potted plant had them, my stuffed gnome on my desk had them, even my computer monitor that I was looking at all day had them! How I did not notice, I do not know. But the kids and I had a good laugh about it once I started finding them around the room.

A HEARTWARMING STORY that will always stick with me is the time that my 3rd grade art class was building three, 4-foot Christmas trees for their Christmas program. There was a boy that struggled in school, academically and socially. He was a quiet kid and did not really say much. He normally struggled in art class too, but with this project something clicked in his brain. He was able to make the base for the tree and attach it to his trunk with ease and faster than the rest of the kids. I walked over to him and said "Wow! You are so smart; you could be a builder one day!" The smile on his face melted my heart because all he ever heard was that he needed to work harder. Any time a student came and asked me to help with their tree I referred them to this student and the smile on his face never left the rest of art class. Since this interaction, I always make a point to find some type of strength in every student and highlight *it* because you never know how much they need that praise.

I WAS TEACHING THIRD GRADE. I needed a pick me up to get me going each day. I would bring Red Bull to school. One day I was sitting and drinking my Red Bull. One of my students walked in and said "I did not know you drank Red Beer!" I quickly explained that I do not drink that. It is Red BULL. This is an energy drink not an alcoholic beverage.

I WAS TEACHING MUSIC to a kindergarten group during Halloween. I love to play pranks in my classes sometimes. During one of the Halloween songs on the projector board, at the end, a skeleton jumps out and says BOO! During the song I snuck to the back of the room with cymbals and hit them together and I made everyone jump. One of the kindergarteners turned around and told me I scared his heart out. It was a very funny moment and I will always talk about it during Halloween.

ONE FALL DAY, we were heading out in front of our school to do an experiment with pumpkins. Minutes before we were to head outside, one of my kindergarten boys had a restroom accident. I sent him to the nurse to get cleaned up and change clothes. When he went to walk out the door, I noticed he had sweatpants on, and I made a mental note to check his pockets before he came back inside. During the experiment I noticed that this particular boy was playing in the rocks. I knew he would have his pockets full of rocks. Of course, he was the last one to come in the door of the building, but I was waiting for him. To my surprise, he did not have any pockets, but his fists were full of rocks. I had him empty his hands. I was very proud of myself for thinking ahead. Back in the classroom, I had the students sitting on my rug and we were discussing Grandparents Day which was the following day. I noticed that my little boy was very "wiggly". He then reaches up his sweat pant leg and pulls something out. He looks at it and throws it at me. I look at the round little "rock" beside my chair and think, "I thought I got all of the rocks out of his hands?" Upon closer inspection, this "rock" was larger and rounder than the ones from outside. That is when it hit me ……… POOP!!!!! One student tried to grab it off of the floor saying, "I'll get it!" I jumped up out of my chair and screamed "DON'T touch it!" The lesson learned is NEVER pick up small, brown objects off of the floor. They are NOT always raisins or rocks!

THANK YOU FOR CHOOSING THE ULTIMATE BEHAVIOR MANAGEMENT MANUAL

It is truly our hope that it helps teachers in their daily quest to educate today's youth.

We are available for keynotes, workshops, and professional development.

If you are interested in our services, please contact us.

Cedar Hills Publishing
19462 Rolling Hills Rd.
Warsaw, Missouri 65355
cedarhillspublishing.com
cedarhillspublishing@gmail.com
660-723-6230

www.ingramcontent.com/pod-product-compliance
Lightning Source LLC
Chambersburg PA
CBHW080736230426
43665CB00020B/2761